Fizz and Buzz

LEVEL 3
/z/zz/

Teaching Tips

Yellow Level 3

This book focuses on the phonemes /z/zz/.

Before Reading
- Discuss the title. Ask readers what they think the book will be about.
- Sound out the words on page 3 together.

Read the Book
- Ask readers to use a finger to follow along with each word as it is read.
- Encourage readers to break down unfamiliar words into units of sound. Then, ask them to string the sounds together to create the words.
- Urge readers to point out when the focused phonics phonemes appear in the text.

After Reading
- Encourage children to reread the book independently or with a friend.
- Ask simple questions about the text to check for understanding. Have them find the pages that have the answers to your questions.

© 2024 Booklife Publishing
This edition is published by arrangement with Booklife Publishing.

North American adaptations © 2024 Jump!
5357 Penn Avenue South
Minneapolis, MN 55419
www.jumplibrary.com

Decodables by Jump! are published by Jump! Library.
All rights reserved. No part of this book may be reproduced in any form without written permission from the publisher.

Library of Congress Cataloging-in-Publication Data is available at www.loc.gov or upon request from the publisher.

ISBN: 979-8-88996-804-7 (hardcover)
ISBN: 979-8-88996-805-4 (paperback)
ISBN: 979-8-88996-806-1 (ebook)

Photo Credits

Images are courtesy of Shutterstock.com. With thanks to Getty Images, Thinkstock Photo and iStockphoto. Cover – ESB Professional. 4–5 – hxdbzxy, YAKOBCHUK VIACHESLAV. 6–7 – Miyao, YAKOBCHUK VIACHESLAV. 8–9 – Krakenimages.com, frantic00. 10–11 – Paolo De Gasperis, frantic00. 14–15 – Shutterstock.

Can you find these words in the book?

buzz

fizz

zags

zap

The lab is all set up.

Can they get it to fizz?

Liz will fill the jar.

They tip it in a big jar and get it to fizz.

Can Zack get it to buzz?

The gas in this will buzz and hum.

Zack taps it. Zap! It zigs and zags.

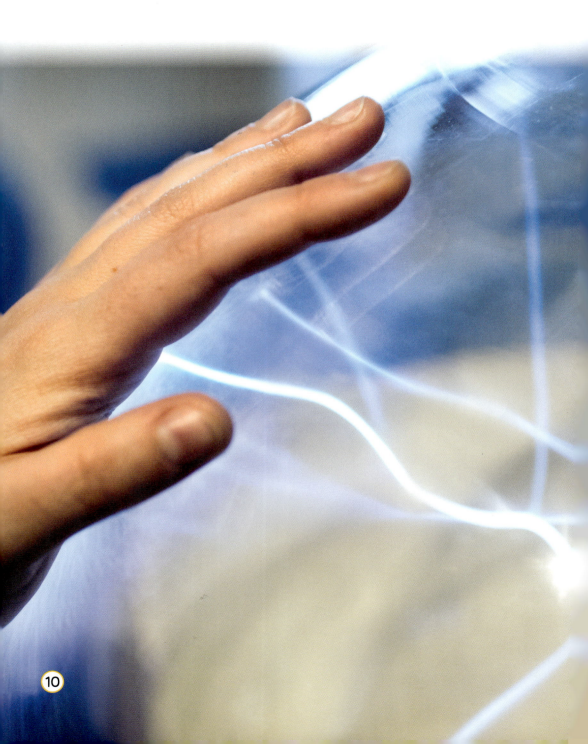

They will all tap it. Buzz, buzz, buzz!

Can you say this sound and draw it with your finger?

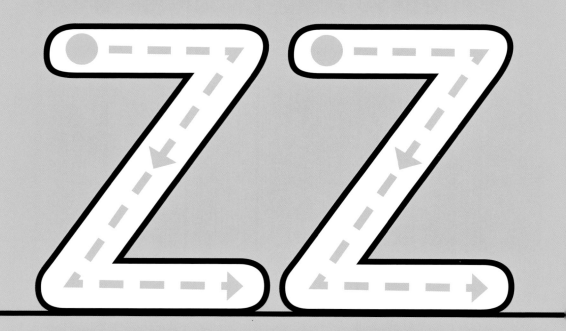

Trace the letter /z/ to complete each word. Say the words out loud.

What other words can you spell with /z/ or /zz/?

__ebra   __ero

si____le

pu___le pi___a

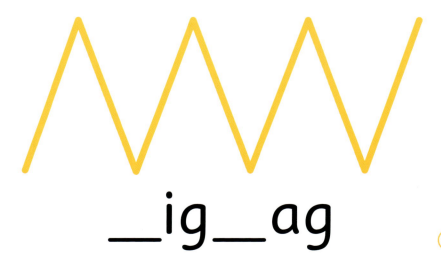

_ig_ag

Practice reading the book again:

The lab is all set up.
Can they get it to fizz?
Liz will fill the jar.
They tip it in a big jar and get it to fizz.
Can Zack get it to buzz?
The gas in this will buzz and hum.
Zack taps it. Zap! It zigs and zags.
They will all tap it. Buzz, buzz, buzz!